How the Colonists Lived

How the Colonists Lived

Arnold Madison

Illustrated by Hameed Benjamin

David McKay Company, Inc.
NEW YORK

Library of Congress Cataloging in Publication Data

Madison, Arnold.
  How the colonists lived.

  Includes index.
  SUMMARY: Text and drawings depict varying aspects of the colonists' lifestyles in the South, New England, and the Mid-Atlantic colonies.
  1. United States—Social life and customs—Colonial period, ca. 1600–1775—Juvenile literature. [1. United States—Social life and customs—Colonial period, ca. 1600–1775] I. Benjamin, Hameed. II. Title.
E162.M26   973.2   80-7968
ISBN 0-679-20685-X

10 9 8 7 6 5 4 3

MANUFACTURED IN THE UNITED STATES OF AMERICA

Contents

Foreword

"Why should we read about something that happened hundreds of years ago? We want to know about *now!*"

This is a comment heard from many young people, and possibly even you have voiced similar feelings. Actually, by studying American history, you are learning more about today. But look at some other reasons first.

The Bicentennial celebration of a few years ago caused many people in the United States to take a keen interest in our history. Those dull facts from textbooks suddenly became vivid, exciting events when we saw battles re-created or a way of life depicted by real people. Although some people lost their curiosity about the past once the Bicentennial ended, others who had gained new insights have continued to build upon them. As a nation, we have become vitally interested in our history.

We are surrounded by physical traces of the American colonists' early years, although many people may be totally unaware of these remains. Few early-morning joggers trotting through the Boston Common appreciate the fact that Boston has that park today because the early colonists set aside land in the center of their settlement for livestock grazing. Nor do many workers scurrying to their jobs in lower Manhattan realize that the erratic street layout of that area has come down to us from the colony of New Amsterdam.

Other elements in our lives—such as foods, holidays, and the designs of some homes—have been influenced by the early colonists. In addition, various parts of our country still reflect the attitudes of the colonists: the fierce individualism of New England, the strict religious feelings in certain parts of Pennsylvania and the Midwest.

Reading about yesterday creates an understanding of today. Where did we first get those doughnuts we enjoy? Why is tobacco a major crop in the South? Why do some areas have blue laws, forcing stores to remain closed on Sunday? All these and many more questions can be answered by delving into the way the colonists lived.

The Southern Colonies

Although evidence appears to support the theory that the Norsemen landed on the shores of Cape Cod, there is no record of their visits, nor did they set up colonies. The first recorded attempt to organize a permanent colony belongs to the French Huguenots.

Fort Caroline

In 1564, the Huguenots arrived in what is now the state of Florida. They erected a triangular palisade on an island in the St. Johns River. Little is known about this first official colony in America other than that the site was named Fort Caroline. One year later, the Spanish attacked and destroyed Fort Caroline. And, as if nature wanted to finish man's destruction, today even the island has been washed away by the river.

St. Augustine

The Spanish who ravaged the Huguenot colony came from

the second official colony to be built in North America. During the mid-1500's, the Spanish created a network of forts to protect their shipping lanes through the Caribbean Sea. St. Augustine, the northernmost fort, was constructed a few miles south of Fort Caroline. The arrival of 600 Spanish settlers marked the beginning of the first *permanent* European colony in the future United States. Although St. Augustine was sacked and burned several times, the colony was rebuilt and is still an important city today. While under Spanish control, however, the colony was viewed only as a protective measure to ensure Spain's superiority on the sea.

Roanoke

The English were the next Europeans to attempt to establish a foothold in the New World; however, in doing so, they created a mystery that may never be solved. In 1584, Sir Walter Raleigh sent an expedition to America. The explorers discovered an island off the coast of present-day North Carolina that appeared suitable for a colony. The report given by Raleigh was glowing:

> . . . a beautiful country, all fair green grass . . . the deer crossing in every path . . . the air fresh . . . and every stone that we stooped to take up promised either silver or gold by complexion.

Queen Elizabeth I knighted Raleigh for the discovery and named the new land Virginia. In 1585 colonists landed on Roanoke, situated in Albemarle Sound. However, because of little support from and contact with their homeland, the colonists became discouraged and returned to England with Sir Francis Drake in 1586.

Meanwhile, another band of colonists was brought to the site by Sir Richard Grenville. Thus began the mystery of Roanoke Island. A year later, 1587, Raleigh sent a larger group

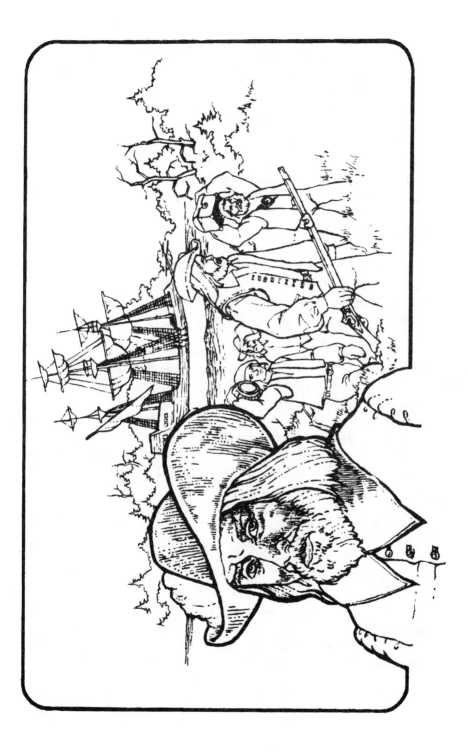

of colonists to the settlement. The 150 colonists, under the command of John White, included twenty-five women and children, the first to come to America from England. But when this third band arrived, they could find no trace of Grenville's colonists. Had they been victims of hostile Indians? Had the men wandered on to settle elsewhere? If so, Grenville's colonists had become lost, because none was ever seen again.

Mystified and frightened by the disappearance of their predecessors, the newcomers nevertheless decided to attempt to create a permanent colony. Living in and around an earth fort approximately fifty feet square, they began farming the rich land.

The leaders wore full suits of armor and flat caps. The armor won appreciative glances from the Indians. The other males dressed in full breeches, or "slops," which were tied at the knee. For the upper portion of the body, a pointed doublet with separate tie-on sleeves was used.

The women also wore doublets, and long skirts that they called petticoats. Their chopines, or shoes, had thick cork soles. Topping off their appearance were close-fitting caps that completely covered their hair.

On August 18, 1587, only weeks after the colonists had disembarked, the first white child of English parents was born in North America. Virginia Dare was John White's granddaughter, and her birth was heralded as a good sign that the latest attempt at colonization would give birth to a growing and successful colony. John White set sail for England with the intention of returning with supplies for the newly established village. Unfortunately, England became involved fighting the Spanish Armada, and Roanoke was neglected. Not until 1591, four years later, was John White able to return to the settlement. A shock awaited him.

Gone. Everything and every settler, including White's own family, had disappeared. The only clue was a word carved into a post, CROATOAN, and forty stone tablets (discovered in 1937) inscribed with what is believed to be the history of the Lost Col-

Male attire featured "slops," full breeches tied at the knee.

ony. Archaeologists who have excavated the site have also discovered some rusted tools, buttons, and buckles.

After the failure of this colony, twenty years would pass before the English attempted to found another colony.

Jamestown

In May 1607 three small ships sailed into Chesapeake Bay, having been at sea for over four months. The people aboard were weary from the long trip, but the sight of the land, cloaked in spring green, inspired them. Also, the dream of the gold they might discover gave them renewed energy. The sailors found a wide river mouth near the southern end of the bay and guided the ships up this river. The new colonists selected a pleasant site for their village.

The colonists had been sent out by the London Company, which received a charter from King James I to create settlements along the coast of what are now Virginia and North Carolina. In honor of their king, the colonists named the river the James and their colony Jamestown.

Foolishly, too many of them wasted precious time searching for gold rather than making preparations for food and shelter. The ever-constant danger of Indians convinced some of the fortune hunters to complete a fort. The triangular structure, built with upright poles, had a fortified area at each corner. For individual shelters within the fort, the colonists used tents—which rotted quickly—or wigwams made with branches.

Unexpected hardships and dangers lurked all around them. Many colonists who drank the brackish river water became ill. The swamps swarmed with mosquitoes, which carried malaria into the Jamestown fort. Food became scarce, because many colonists were digging for gold rather than planting fields with corn. Even worse, the men in the group were unaccustomed to physical labor and were inappropriately dressed. Some had even brought starch with them to keep the ruffs on their doublets stiff. Disappointed that their dreams of wealth had proven

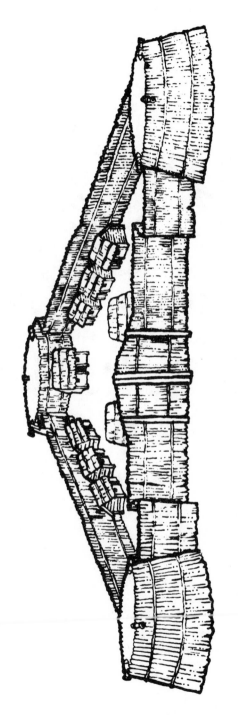

Jamestown Fort.

Wattle and daub cabin.

futile and wearied by the rigors of harsh living, the colonists settled down to a desperate struggle to survive. By autumn of 1607, barely one-third of the settlers were still alive.

The colony's savior was Captain John Smith. When the success of Jamestown seemed very dim, Smith took firm control. He instituted a "no work, no food" rule. Even the laziest man soon contributed his muscle power for the good of the colony. Food crops were planted, and more substantial housing was constructed within the fort.

Ironically, these men, used to genteel living, built a type of house the peasants of Europe had inhabited for centuries. The first "cabbins" in Jamestown were constructed by resting a thatched roof on forked posts. The walls were vertical stakes, a few inches apart, woven together horizontally with willow or hazel leaves. The empty spaces in the walls were filled with a mixture of mud and straw, called "wattle and daub." The cabin had no chimney, merely an open hole in the ceiling through which the smoke of the cooking fire escaped.

Smith also organized an industry. Since there was no gold to send back to the parent London Company, the colonists had to export some products. Smith decided to manufacture clapboards, because this method of siding the outside of buildings was popular in England. Clapboards were made from logs about ten inches thick. The worker used a froe, an instrument resembling a wide wedge, with a straight, heavy blade and a handle attached at a right angle. Standing a log on end, a man hammered the froe until the wood split in half. The two halves were then repeatedly split until all that remained were boards about five-eighths-inch thick on one edge, narrowing down to a sharp point on the other side. The clapboards were approximately five inches wide and four feet long.

For the next two years, Jamestown continued to barely eke out an existence. Under Smith's guidance, crops were planted, food was shared, and Indians were controlled. The people survived from one day to the next. In 1609, however, Smith was badly burned in a gunpowder explosion. He went back to En-

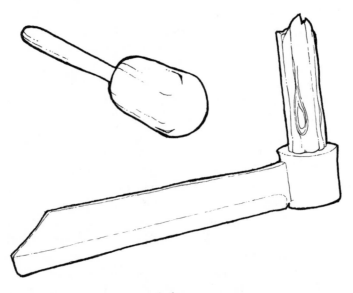

A froe.

gland for treatment and never returned to Virginia. With Smith's strong rule gone, Jamestown began to deteriorate. In fact, food was so scarce during the winter of 1609–1610 that the period was known as the "starving time." When spring finally came, only sixty men were alive. Thoroughly disheartened, they boarded ships for the return to England. However, as the vessels reached the mouth of the James River, the men saw boats bringing supplies and more colonists. Everyone sailed to Jamestown.

That moment was the lowest point for the colony. With the arrival of the much-needed supplies and new colonists, a fresh determination took hold. The original colonists had learned from their mistakes and could guide the newcomers. And, because many of the incoming colonists were skilled in carpentry and other useful trades, more comfortable homes were built.

Now logs were squared and fitted together or secured with homemade wooden pegs. Iron nails were scarce. Therefore, if a man moved or constructed a new home, he would burn down his old house to retrieve the nails. The empty spaces between the logs or planks were packed with moss or wattle and daub. The doors were a double layer of rough planks, hung on wooden hinges. Should there be a window in the door or, more likely, in the wall, the opening was situated high above the floor for good ventilation and protection. If iron nails were scarce, glass was even more rare. Paper soaked in linseed oil was set into the window frame, giving the building's interior a gloomy appearance because the translucent paper allowed only a little light to enter. These newer homes had chimneys that were constructed away from the wall, at the room's far end. This design was used because setting the chimney out from the wall reduced the danger of fire. Also, the climate was mild, and only a little heat was needed.

Furniture had to be made from cut trees, so only the most essential pieces were found in the Jamestown cabins. The head of the family often had a chair, but other members had to use benches or stools. Tables for eating were set up by placing planks on trestles. After each meal, they were dismantled to create more space. In sharp contrast to the simple furniture was the large, curtained bed. The English colonists were accustomed to sleeping behind heavy drapes, so the custom was carried to the New World.

The arrival of the latest wave of colonists not only raised the spirits of the surviving Jamestown veterans, but also seemed to signal an immediate change in the colony's prosperity. In that same year, 1610, a discovery was made that would eventually bring more money to Virginia than even the naive gold hunters had envisioned. The source was the soil. The product was not mineral, however, but rather a plant.

After his voyage to the New World, Raleigh had introduced the practice of smoking to England. Between 1600 and 1625 the most discussed topic in that country was whether or not to smoke. Many people believed smoking was harmful. Some claimed that smoking dried up a person's brain and wasted his body. In 1604, King James I labeled smoking a "vile and stinking custome." But it was a custom that grew, and with it grew the demand for the tobacco leaf.

In an effort to find a marketable product, the Jamestown colonists had tried growing tobacco. However, the crop was poor and biting in taste. In 1612, however, John Rolfe experimented with tobacco plants grown in Cuba. This variety adapted well to the Virginia soil and climate. Three years later, Rolfe sent his first shipment to England, where the tobacco sold quickly. By 1618, Virginia was selling more tobacco than Spain and its colonies—formerly the largest tobacco producers. Jamestown had found its means to survive and flourish.

Tobacco mania swept the colony. Everybody started planting tobacco—even in the streets of Jamestown. Imported craftsmen had been brought to Jamestown to organize factories for the production of glass, wine, and silk. The workers fled to the fields, and the factories closed down. The tobacco plant itself was used as money. Public officials and clergymen were paid with tobacco rather than currency.

The newfound success had an immediate effect on the colonists' life-style. Because tobacco-growing requires large fields, the farmers had to abandon the village concept, in which houses are grouped closely, and move to homes surrounded by miles of open land. But once a planter found himself on one of these isolated farms, he lacked the services of a blacksmith or a carpenter, who were readily available in a town. Slowly, the plantation way of life, characteristic of the South for the next 200 years, evolved. Each farm became a small village in itself.

But the tobacco growers did not begin with vast plantations. The men moved into small cabins even more crude than the ones they had left in Jamestown. No time was available for creating furnishings other than the barest essentials. The tobacco fields demanded the farmer's every moment.

Prosperity brought even more changes. As the farmer's crops began to sell, he would become dissatisfied with his simple cabin. Now he wanted a two-story, rectangular brick house with a chimney at each end. The sloping roof would have dormer windows to permit light to enter the two upstairs sleeping rooms. Downstairs, the two rooms had casement windows that opened outward, like miniature doors, and held diamond-shaped panes of imported glass. For the more successful grower, the inside walls might be plastered with clay and whitened with lime made from oyster shells. Gone were the roughly hewn slabs of furniture. They were replaced by tables and chairs imported from England. The early wooden tableware was also discarded, and the family ate their meals from utensils of pewter, a metal composed of tin and lead. The old cabin was converted into a separate kitchen, and the food was served in the dining room of the main house.

As improved as the living conditions were, the new houses still reflected the fact that these farmers were colonists in another people's land. As the plantations spread, devouring forest

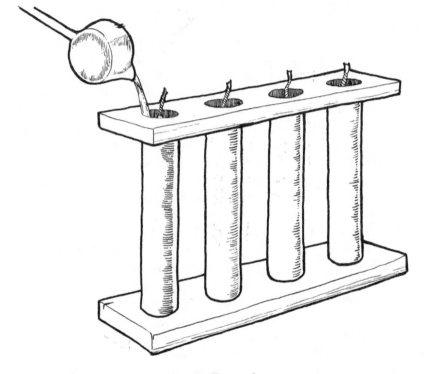

A candle-maker.

land and spewing out tobacco fields, the Native Americans in Virginia became increasingly hostile. Where were the forests that had provided their food, clothing, and shelter? In addition, many white colonists were incredibly arrogant when dealing with the Indians. Therefore, the new plantation homes were built with loopholes in the second story, through which a rifle might be fired. Some houses had hidden spaces between the walls near the fireplaces, called "hideyholes." Some were even equipped with underground tunnels through which the plantation owner and his family could flee to a nearby river or safe refuge.

Another need was evident as the plantations prospered and the owners' lives became easier. The huge tracts of land and buildings needed people to work them. By order of the king, one hundred convicts were removed from English prisons and sent to the colony, where they were sold as bonded servants. Usually their time of bondage was five years, after which they were freed. Some eventually became landowners and successful farmers themselves. The boatloads of convicts who arrived steadily during the next one hundred years eased the problem. But the fields needed workers—many, many unpaid workers.

In 1619 a Dutch trading vessel brought a cargo of twenty black natives from Africa to Jamestown. At first, the blacks were not viewed as slaves, but merely as bonded servants—the same as the English criminals. Some were destined to be granted freedom. By 1662, however, the slave concept was born from economic necessity. The plantation owners could not afford to continually purchase new bonded servants. Now the blacks were brought as personal belongings of the landowner, to do with as he wished. Some slaves fared well, either because they were a financial investment and therefore the owner had to keep them healthy, or because they were acquired by kind people. Many slaves, however, were treated as livestock; their families were wrenched apart and scattered throughout the South. From childhood to old age, hundreds of slaves worked all facets of the townlike plantations with never a hope of being freed.

Almost every plantation had slaves operating a brickyard. A preference for brick buildings made supplies of new bricks constant necessities. At times, tobacco plantations sold bricks to provide supplementary income. A kiln was set up close to a clay bank so that firewood and water were available. Clay was dug and placed in a pit for about a week, while water was poured continually over the material.

The next step was to shovel the clay into a "pugmill," a container similar to a large vat. Standing perpendicular in the vat was a thick post with protruding metal pins. This pole was connected to another, which was pulled by an ox or a horse. As the post equipped with the pins revolved, the spikes mixed the clay with more water, turning it into the consistency of smooth bread dough. The pins were also arranged so that they forced the clay downward, squeezing it through a tiny opening in the bottom.

While one slave dumped new clay and water into the pugmill, another stood in a pit by the opening. He would roll a lump of the freshly mixed clay in sand and press it into a wooden mold. The mold, too, had already been soaked and dipped in sand. The sand permitted the bricks to be easily removed from the mold, which had slots for four to eight bricks. When each space had been filled and the top of the clay scraped flat, the blocks were dumped onto a board. Then they would dry in the air for several weeks.

Next, the bricks were baked in kilns for ten days. The dried, molded bricks were stacked to form long tunnels inside the kiln. An opening led into the tunnel at each end. The blocks were set so that their shorter ends, or "headers," faced the tunnel, where fires had been built. Fire also raged within the kiln walls. The heat given off by the burning hard oak was so intense that the headers of the bricks close to the fire were transformed into rough glass with a bluish, shiny surface. When these bricks were later used in construction, the bricklayer arranged them in an

16

alternating pattern. First, he would set a brick so that the long side showed; then one was placed so only the header was visible. By doing this, a pattern of red and blue, known as Flemish bond, was created.

While several slaves worked the brickyard, others operated the sawmill. These sawmills, which were either water- or wind-powered, provided a constant supply of planking for the carpenter's shop and the building crews on the plantation. A blacksmith shop produced metal implements and shoes for the horses, and a cobbler's shop made shoes for the owner's family and plantation workers.

Other buildings were situated on the self-sufficient plantation. A spinning house, weaving house, and schoolhouse all provided goods and services. The owner's sons were tutored privately and were expected to learn the tobacco trade firsthand by working and overseeing various sectors of the plantation. The daughters received only enough formal education to allow them to efficiently manage the household and entertain guests.

One of the most important aspects of daily life on a plantation was the preparation and serving of meals in the main house. As mentioned earlier, when the prospering plantation owner moved into a larger home, the smaller house was converted into a kitchen. At first, this was done merely to save space in the new house. But then the wisdom of such an arrangement was noted. The warm Southern climate provided enough (often too much) heat for the owner's house, and the building certainly did not need additional warmth from cooking fireplaces. So, kitchens were purposely built separately, although some had connecting passageways to the owner's house.

The daily routine in the planter's house was different from the one most Americans observe today. The owner would rise early and drink a glass of beer made from corn. In addition to the money crop, all plantations had cornfields to provide food for the family. After his morning beer, the owner left with his overseer to inspect the crops and work crews.

About ten o'clock he returned for a large breakfast of beef

17

or turkey. Hens had not yet been trained to produce regularly, so eggs were a rarity. In fact, they were so scarce that they were saved and served as a party delicacy. Meat, prepared for breakfast and the other meals, had a strong, salty taste because the only way it could be preserved was by salting or smoking.

After breakfast, the plantation owner concerned himself with business matters related to his land, crops, and workers or else he devoted time to his family. Dinner was served at about three-thirty or four o'clock in the afternoon. The owner expected and received bountiful meals. Platters of fish, fowl, oysters, beef, and crabs were set on the table alongside many kinds of vegetables. Corn bread was heated in the kitchen or lifted right from the baking utensil and rushed by a running slave to the dining room. Leftovers from these banquet-like dinners were given to the servants working in the kitchen or sent to the slaves' quarters. For some blacks, this provided a change from their almost constant diet of terrapin—a water turtle that crawls on land.

The time between dinner and supper, or a light meal eaten at about nine o'clock at night, was called evening, although we would refer to part of those hours as late afternoon. A planter's evening might be spent again giving attention to business or else occupied with socializing. The family retired after supper, unless the meal had become a party. The famous "Southern hospitality" was born in Jamestown because there was a realistic need to be served.

Living such an isolated life, plantation families were eager to receive people and especially news of what was happening in the world beyond the colony. Such information could only be brought by letter or by word of mouth, for there were no newspapers.

Travel from one plantation to another was accomplished mostly by boat. At first there were few roads, but even after some roads had been constructed, people still used boats, because water travel was faster than land travel. The shore of Chesapeake Bay was so indented with inlets that plantations separated by less than a mile of water could only be reached on land by traveling many miles. So, plantation owners often stationed slaves near the water or by the road, if there was one. Any passersby or boats filled with people were hailed and invited for food and drink and, at times, even for an overnight stay. This practice evoked many complaints from the innkeepers, whose business was hurt by the generous Southern hospitality.

Not only did the social life, homes, and meals reflect the colonists' success, but also their clothing and fashions grew steadily more fancy. Now ships from England carried the finest cloth and perfumes to the Jamestown docks.

When not overseeing the business, the plantation men wore velvet or satin waistcoats with embroidered flowers, double rows of gold buttons, lace, and ruffles. Knee-length breeches, white silk stockings, and shoes with large red heels and paste buckles completed the outfit.

European hairstyles for men also reached the shores of Chesapeake Bay, where they were quickly adopted. Hot, heavy, uncomfortable wigs became the rage. Styles constantly changed from long, curly periwigs to puffy white wigs with long braids hanging down the back. In the Southern climate, such wigs were most unpleasant to wear, and the men added to their discomfort by powdering their wigs with a chalky white dust. This not only choked the person applying the powder but also marred the appearance of the fancy clothing, because a draft or breeze caused the powder to swirl around the man's head like a miniature dust storm.

Resting on the masses of powdered hair were large hats. With the passage of time, the hat brims grew wider and wider. Soon, one side of the brim had to be tacked up so the man could see. Then another part was connected to the top. Finally, when the third portion of the brim was hooked, the famous three-cornered "cocked hat" had entered colonial fashion.

As if to match the ever-widening brims of men's hats, women's skirts billowed out further and further. Large hoop frames extended the fancy skirts to a distance of four feet. As a result, a special chair with no arms had to be devised so that women could sit down.

The Jamestown women also became addicted to accessories. They had so many gadgets and ornaments, they lacked space to carry or hang them. One favorite ornament was the patchbox, a container made with silver and ivory or tortoiseshell. Inside the tiny lid was a mirror that enabled a woman to see exactly where to place the black "beauty spot" on her face. This same face needed protection from sunlight, so whenever a woman went outside or traveled, she held a linen or velvet mask to her face. Gold accessories—rings, lockets, and buckles—were acquired. Delicate silk-and-lace handkerchiefs were carried or attached to clothing. From the woman's waist hung a small "etui," an ornamental pouch containing a tiny pair of scissors, thread, and other objects.

However, it was the fan that was to reach its moment of glory in the hands of the Jamestown women. The fans, made of either carved ivory or fluffy peacock feathers, became extensions of the bearers. In a type of body language, the skilled Southern woman could communicate pleasure, dismay, and other subtle emotions with a single gesture of her fan.

Possibly, the female's absorption in so many accessories limited her interest in hats. Often, the head garb was little more than a hood. A quote from the journal of Philip Fithian, a young Northerner who came to Virginia to tutor the children of a plantation owner, described his reaction:

> . . . it is a custom among the ladies, whenever they go from home, to muffle up their heads and necks, leaving only a narrow passage for the eyes, in cotton or silk handkerchiefs; I was in distress for them when I first came into the colony, for every woman that I saw abroad I looked upon as ill either with the mumps or toothache!

Philip Fithian might well have been concerned about the

health of the Jamestown colonists, because that area of every-day living did not improve along with other aspects of life.

Dentists simply did not exist, and, in fact, people did not realize that tooth decay could be prevented or eliminated. A rotting tooth merely decayed until the point when the pain became unbearable. Then the strongest man on the plantation was employed to pull it out. In towns, barbers or blacksmiths would do this service for a fee. Most Jamestown residents had lost all their teeth by the time they reached thirty.

Medical attention was equally poor. What few doctors there were in the colony were thought to be about as effective as a Native American's medicine man. People relied on home remedies and luck. And, too often, the luck ran out. Infant mortality was extremely high. Even if a person did survive the early years, the twenties and thirties often proved fatal. If a person lived to the age of fifty, he or she probably had been married twice. The individual who could reel off the names of five mates, all of whom had passed away, was not unusual. On the plantations the grim task of building the coffins fell to the carpentry shop. The coffins were constructed to exact measurements and had the shape of a human body. Burial was swift because even these people, with their limited medical knowledge, realized that disease spread swiftly from decaying bodies in the Southern heat.

Death, however, was not to be Jamestown's major contribution to our heritage, but rather birth. Not the birth of the tobacco industry, but the genesis of an idea that would spread and, in time, bring an end to the entire colonial era.

The Jamestown Colony had been organized and settled under the direction of the London Company. For a period of time, men selected by that company ruled the colony. In 1619, however, the colony was permitted to choose representatives from its own population to help make laws for the colony. The governing body was called the House of Burgesses. Persons from all parts of Virginia attended a two-week session in Williamsburg twice a year. There the representatives discussed the laws and voiced the opinions of the colonists who had elected them. Years later, the first sentiments against taxation without representation would be voiced in this assembly, and Patrick Henry would present his famous "Give me liberty or give me death" speech.

Even more important, this first form of representative government in America would kindle the concept of democracy, which would sweep all the colonies and bring about the creation of the United States. For that contribution alone, we all should be grateful to the hardworking colonists of Jamestown.

2

The New England Colonies

Although the first Southern colonies were settled for military and economic gain, the original New England colonies were the result of a quest for religious freedom. Perhaps this would have to be the reason for selecting that portion of North America where the climate and land itself were not as receptive as the mild weather and rich soil of the Southern colonies.

Plymouth

Ironically, the Pilgrims who landed in Plymouth, Massachusetts, thought they were headed for Virginia. The captain of the *Mayflower* made a miscalculation that he refused to rectify. But his error caused another example where a self-rule policy was already part of the colonists' life.

Pilgrims were actually Separatists, a group that wished to be separated from the Church of England and worship as it wished. Having been persecuted in England, the Pilgrims fled to Holland, where they hoped to find peace. Although these people wanted to be free of the Church of England, they did not want to desert their English ways. The language and customs of Holland were strange to them, and, even worse, their children were emulating the Dutch. Also, in England the Separatists had been farmers, and now they were forced to live in cities.

Arrangements were made with the London Company to settle on land the company owned in North America. To do so, the Pilgrims had to sign an agreement to send everything they produced for the next seven years to the London Company. This did not include the supplies they themselves needed. On September 6, 1620, the *Mayflower* sailed from Plymouth, England, with 149 people aboard. Its destination was Virginia.

On November 9 the sailors spotted Cape Cod and sailed into the harbor of what is now Provincetown. The ship's captain, apparently feeling that one part of the New World was as good as any other, would not sail on to Virginia. His decision placed the Pilgrims in a quandary. The land they would be settling was not under the jurisdiction of the London Company.

Several Pilgrim leaders met in the ship's small cabin and drew up the Mayflower Compact, which, in effect, provided that leaders would be elected to make laws for the new colony.

> In the name of God, Amen. We whose names are underwritten . . . having undertaken . . . a voyage to plant the first colony in the northern parts of Virginia, do . . . solemnly (agree) to enact . . . such just and equal laws . . . from time to time, as shall be thought (best) for the general good of the Colony, unto which we promise all . . . obedience.

On December 11, 1620, an exploration party from the *Mayflower* landed at what now is Plymouth and inspected the area. Because the site seemed the best along the bleak shore, the *Mayflower* brought the Pilgrims to Plymouth five days later. Although the captain had refused to continue on to Virginia, he agreed to remain in the harbor so the boat might be used as a base of operations.

The most urgent problem facing the new colonists was to provide shelter from the winter, which was already upon them. The first homes were literally holes in the ground covered with bark roofs supported on poles. On Christmas Day the building of the first house for common use was begun. The word *common* was to be an important one that first year in Plymouth. The land was to be shared by all in common—all would work and all would share.

During the next few months, over half the group perished from cold, hunger, and disease. When spring came, only fifty survivors remained in Plymouth. However, these people knew they had the freedom to worship, as well as govern themselves, so they decided to stay. On April 5, 1621, the *Mayflower* sailed for England.

As time went on, life became more bearable in Plymouth. Friendly Native Americans taught the colonists how to hunt, fish, and plant corn. The importance of corn to all the colonies cannot be overemphasized. This one item was probably the single reason that the colonists lived long enough to succeed in their colonization attempts.

During the first year, Plymouth encountered problems with its common-land policy. Those who worked hard objected because the lazier colonists were getting an equal share. Although the original Thanksgiving was held to celebrate the harvest of the first planting of corn and squash, dissension ended the common-land practice. During the second year, lots were parceled out to each family. This procedure worked well because each family knew that it would have to live on what it produced.

On November 10, 1621, the *Fortune* arrived at Plymouth with thirty-five new colonists but no supplies. Sixty-five more people stepped ashore in the spring of 1622. The colonists hovered on the brink of starvation until the new crops could be harvested. That they survived at all can again be attributed to the help provided by the Indians. They taught the colonists how to find the New England clam at low tide. The state of Massachu-

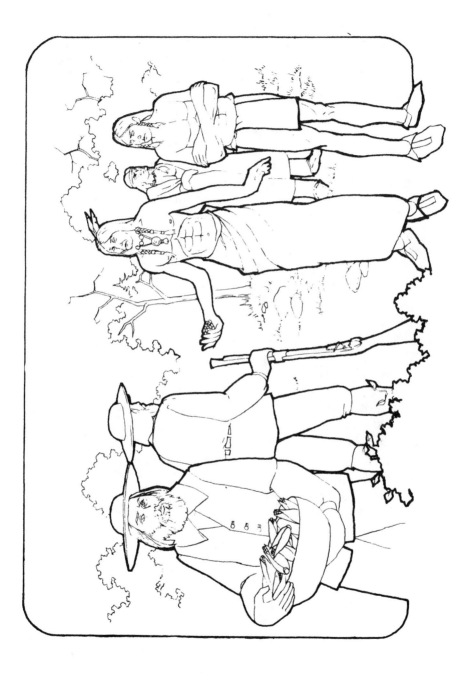

setts has expressed gratitude to the codfish, which over the years provided food and income to that state's residents. In fact, there is even a model of a codfish hanging in a state building. But there are some people who feel more acknowledgment should be given to the lowly clam, which kept the Pilgrims alive until their second harvest—a bountiful one.

Under the guidance of Governor William Bradford, the colony now flourished. Famine never again threatened the people. Also, by the end of the first year, seven homes had been built. One year later, the colonists had left their crowded, smoky holes in the ground for small timber cottages.

Their clothing was simple, also. A misconception exists about the Pilgrims' garb that has no historical accuracy but nevertheless seems unshakable. They did *not* dress in black and white. Taste ran toward tans, rusty reds, and browns. The men wore soft caps or wide-brimmed hats with low crowns. Their white shirts were linen, partially covered by a plain leather jerkin or sleeveless jacket. Full leather breeches met woolen stockings. Because boots were so costly, the men wore low shoes tied with a latchet, or leather strap.

Some historians believe the Pilgrim women wore high-crowned hats. If this is accurate, we can assume they also wore "head rails," or hoods, under the hats. Two other articles of clothing were almost a uniform for Pilgrim women. First, they wore a white neckcloth over a simple doublet. The second piece of apparel, without which no woman would be seen in public, was a large apron covering her full skirt.

Both male and female clothing typified the colony: it was functional. The people were down-to-earth and had to devote most of their attention to simply living from day to day. The colony of Plymouth grew in strength until it became a dominant force in New England, but it remained relatively small for all its power.

Massachusetts Bay

Another English religious group was inspired by the success of the Pilgrims and their Plymouth colony. These people did not wish to separate from the Church of England but merely to purify certain portions of the religion. Thus, they became known as the Puritans, who, like the Separatists, were persecuted throughout England.

Most Puritans were well-to-do, middle-class people who belonged to a trading company similar to the London Company. The Massachusetts Bay Company owned a charter from the king and land in the Old World. When the Puritans decided to migrate to America, they bought out the members who wished to remain in the New World. On March 29, 1630, eleven ships containing 900 Puritans set sail. They arrived in present-day Salem harbor on June 12. This group was followed quickly by others, and by the end of the first summer 2,000 colonists were living in and around what is now the city of Boston.

From the very beginning, this band of colonists was more organized and better equipped than either the Jamestown or Plymouth colonists. They did not live in caves or holes like the Pilgrims. Using the lodge of Native Americans as a prototype, the Puritans built rectangular houses with arched roofs. The pole frames were lashed together with vines. Bark and matting covered the skeleton. Rather than a smoke hole in the ceiling, like the original lodge, these communal homes had chimneys made of sticks and clay. Unfortunately, the chimneys were not sturdy and frequently caught fire. However, the frame structures were to be only temporary homes.

Almost as soon as the lodge-type buildings were completed, the Puritan families were hard at work on one-room cabins—their permanent homes. Even though the Puritans had brought ample supplies, many materials were scarce or nonexistent, so they often had to improvise. For example, many Puritan cabins had door hinges and bolts made from the wood of the holly tree.

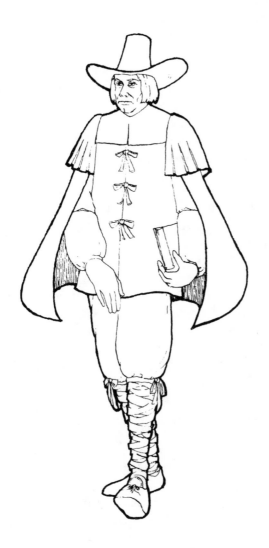

Also, oiled paper filled the window frames. This makeshift glass was covered with animal skins during the winter to seal out the freezing wind.

The main features of the low dwelling were the fireplace and chimney, built into a corner to conserve heat. A fire burned constantly, summer and winter, for several reasons. Heat, light, and cooking purposes were served; also, once the fire died, it was difficult to start a new one. Each family had the flint and steel needed, but often sent a youngster scurrying to a neighbor to borrow a bucket of hot coals.

In another corner rested a platform, which served as a bed when a mattress of feather straw was thrown upon the top. Shoved underneath the platform was a smaller bed, called a trundle bed. The name derived from the fact that the bed could be "trundled" under the platform during the day to save space. Trundle beds were used by children.

Other furniture, arranged around the hearth, included a handmade cradle, a spinning wheel, and a "settle," or high-backed bench.

To solve the problem of illuminating the cabin at night, the colonists lit pine knots containing a resin that burned with a clear light. Unfortunately, the "candle-wood" emitted thick smoke and dropped bits of melted pitch. The problem was solved by inserting the knots into the stones of the fireplace. All grease and fat was saved for use in "betty lamps," which were metal, saucer-like containers that hung from chains. As conditions improved and more fat became available, tallow candles were used to light the cabins.

When these individual homes were being constructed, a pattern for what is now the typical New England village was devised. The center area of the colony was set aside as common pastureland for all the colonists. Appropriately, this area was called the common. Years later, when pastureland was used outside the village, the common remained as a park and the center of village life. Present-day residents of Boston can thank the Puritans for their beautiful park—the Boston Common, originally a pasture.

The land surrounding the common was divided into lots. The most important people in the colony received parcels facing the common; the ordinary citizen had to find land wherever he could for his family's home and farm.

The one building that was always placed by the common was the meetinghouse. Nothing was more important in Puritan life than religion. Even when they were struggling to survive, the Puritans' uppermost thought was to obey God. They believed they had been chosen by God for a special purpose. Their zeal was so intense that this group, which had left England because of persecution, in turn permitted no religious freedom in its own colony. Individuals who followed a different religion, such as the Quakers, were beaten, branded, and even hung.

Obviously, the Sabbath—Sunday—was a most important day. Nothing was allowed to interfere with worship and the Lord's word on that day. Therefore, preparations for Sunday were completed on Saturday, before sundown. All the meals for the next day, as well as the clothing to be worn, were prepared ahead. Stiff fines awaited any person who violated the Sabbath. Considering the fact that two shillings was a typical day's wage, the penalty of three shillings because a child played at the Sabbath meeting was harsh. Even more so was the forty-shilling fine for singing, running, or jumping on the Sabbath. These "blue laws," which are still in effect in some states, fine businesses that operate on Sunday, and are direct descendants of the Puritans' beliefs.

Early on Sunday morning a signal, such as a drum roll, gunshot, or horn, called all the families to the meetinghouse. The early meeting halls had no bells. Inside the bare building were plain wooden benches, upon which the men sat on one side and the women on the other. The minister would open with a prayer that lasted for at least an hour. After the lengthy prayer, the congregation rose for the psalm. In an effort to cleanse the

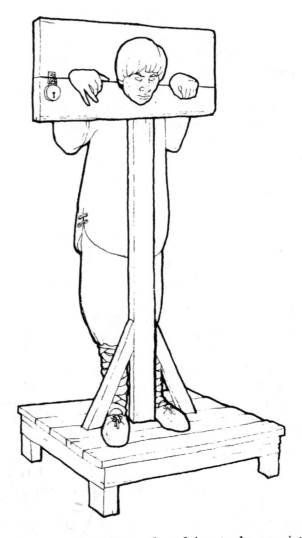

An offender was sometimes placed in stocks consisting of a wooden frame with holes in which the feet and hands were confined.

Church of England, the Puritans did not allow music during a religious service. Rather, a deacon conducted the "lining of the psalm" by reading one line of the psalm, which the congregation in turn droned in unison.

The sermon followed the psalm. The people sat on the hard, wooden benches while the minister preached fire-and-brimstone sermons depicting the terrible evils of sin. Clearly, there were many sins and punishments, for while the minister ranted, sand trickled through an hourglass on the pulpit. With a quick flick of his wrist, the minister would swing the hourglass as the sands ran out. Inspired preachers could continue for as long as four hours.

Not only might the young children become restless, but even some adults grew sleepy. An ever-watchful "tithingman" was on duty. He carried a long pole that had a feather or squirrel's tail on one end and a solid, round knob on the other. Ladies who began to nod would be awakened by a tickling of the feather. Repeaters or soundly sleeping—possibly snoring—men felt the jab of the knob.

Noontime permitted those who lived nearby to return home for their midday meal. Worshipers who lived too far away would retire to a specially built Sabbath house for their meal. The break was a short one, however, and soon everyone was back on the hard benches for an afternoon session—as long and oratorical as the morning meeting. At day's end, each family went home and spent the evening discussing the sermons of the Sabbath.

The religious view that the Devil was literally afoot among the people, and had to be denied in every way, made possible one of the most disgraceful events in the history of the United States: the Salem Witch-Hunt. The Puritans had a fanatical belief in witches. Slowly, at first, men and women were convicted as witches and hung. The "witch" might be an old woman who talked to her cat, or another woman who walked along a muddy road without getting splashed. The first person fell under suspicion because witches were supposed to have animals who were "familiars" and did their evil work. Another person might see the woman successfully travel the muddy road and decide the devil had carried her over the mud. As silly as these explanations may sound to us today, the Puritans accepted the guilt of these individuals and hung them.

The climax of the witch-hunt came in Salem during 1692. Based on testimony from a few hysterical children, the court sentenced nineteen "witches" to death. The death of the nineteen people stunned the inhabitants of New England. Later, the judge himself confessed that he doubted the guilt of the imagined witches. Even more distressing evidence surfaced. The Puritan leaders had staged the trials in a desperate attempt to keep control over the people of Salem, because many non-Puritans were now living there. The needless deaths had been caused by politicians who felt their rule being undermined. This sad period in history came to an end, although many people continued to believe in witches. Today, the term witch-hunt means to persecute or defame a person to gain a political advantage.

During the early days of the Massachusetts Bay Colony, the Puritans' clothing reflected their strict view of life. The men wore wide-brimmed hats, black doublets with simple white collars, baggy breeches, stockings, and square-cut shoes. A woman's apparel consisted of a long-sleeved dress with neckerchief and a white linen apron. Whenever she went outdoors, a Puritan female wore a kerchief or hood to cover her head.

Other rules regulated the clothing. Because certain Englishmen, who had not followed the Puritan religion, made extensive use of buttons for decoration, the Puritans tried to eliminate every button possible. Loops and ties were devised to keep articles of clothing connected. Also, points were used. These were long rows of short strings or tapes attached to the opposite edges of a garment. The end of the points were fashioned with metal tags or tassels, which were tied together to hold the pieces in place.

However, everything about Puritan clothing and life was

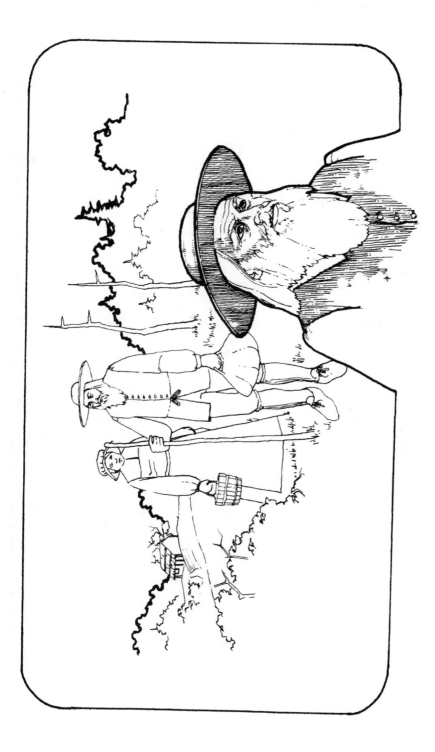

not drab. For example, the Puritans enjoyed the use of colors in their garments. Women dyed their homespun cloth with what they called the "sad" colors: brown, dull green, and purple. Some men wore green cotton waistcoats and red hats. Also, festive occasions marked the Puritans' day. Although they scorned any entertainment that might be frivolous or worldly, they thoroughly enjoyed get-togethers that were functional as well as fun. Neighbors would congregate for a house-raising, much as future farmers would join together in efforts to build a neighbor's barn. There were stone-haulings, corn-huskings, and apple-paring parties. After the serious work was accomplished, a time of happy conversation, eating cakes and pies, and drinking cider and rum followed. The Puritans, for all their religious inflexibility, were healthy eaters and heavy drinkers. A Puritan family—including the children—would start their day with a "morning draft" of beer or ale. Later, because of the plentiful supply of apples, the morning drink became hard cider.

Mealtime saw the man of the house and his older sons sitting at the table, still wearing their hats. Full-time wearing of hats—even in church—was common at this time. If there was a "serving wench" or an older daughter who could bring the food, the wife sat beside her husband rather than at the opposite end of the table. Younger children stood at the table and sometimes at a separate table, eating whatever they were given and not speaking a word during the meal.

Although some families merely placed the cooking pot on the table for everyone to eat directly from the container, most people had utensils. A wooden trencher served as a plate. A trencher was generally rectangular in shape—merely a piece of wood with the center hollowed out. Two diners shared one trencher. Each person had a linen napkin, because everyone ate with their fingers. If the food was too soupy, spoons were used or the liquid was sopped up with pieces of bread. No knives were placed on the table, because each man and older boy had a sheathed knife at his waist. This could be extracted and passed

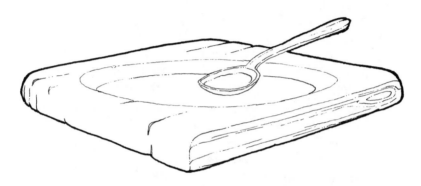

A wooden trencher and spoon.

around when needed. Also on the table were wooden noggins or pewter tankards for either milk, beer, or cider.

Seasonings such as salt depended upon the family's economic level. Salt was expensive, because most of the supply was imported from Spain and Africa's Cape Verde Islands. Honey was the common sweetener, although Native Americans had taught the colonists how to boil down maple sap and make sugar. In years to come, the colonists would import molasses and then cane sugar. That substance would be sold in solid, beehive-shaped lumps, which had to be broken into smaller bits for use. Bread, too, was broken from loaves rather than sliced. No butter was used by the New England colonists.

At the conclusion of a meal, a voider, or basket, was passed around the table for all the utensils and napkins. The soiled items were washed later. First, the entire family, including the wife and older children, enjoyed an after-dinner smoke. Tobacco was placed in clay pipes and lit from the fire. Small tweezers, called smoking tongs, were used to lift a hot ember from the fireplace into a clay pipe.

As the years passed, the Massachusetts Bay Colony, which had begun with a larger number of people than Plymouth, grew more rapidly than its neighbor. However, changes were taking place in that strong colony. Offshoot settlements in what would become Rhode Island and Connecticut were set up to escape the religious persecution in the Bay Colony. And, as evidenced by the Salem witch trials, the Puritan leaders were losing their tight control over the people. In 1691, the Massachusetts Bay Colony united with Plymouth to form a single colony named Massachusetts.

Various religions had now spread throughout New England, but the traditional appearance of the towns was altered only slightly. The starkly constructed Puritan meetinghouse was often converted into a church for another sect. A steeple containing a bell was added, and the building was painted white. Even new towns with no meetinghouses, dating back to

Puritan use, observed the custom of setting their churches on the common.

The steeple bell now became a means of communication for the small towns. On Sunday the bell summoned church-goers to a much less vigorous service than the Puritans had endured. There were still two services every Sunday, but the hours-long, haranguing sermons were gone forever. Hymns were sung in a mood that was equally religious and more bearable.

During the week, the church bell alerted field workers that dinner time had arrived. Less happy news, such as a death, was also spread by the tolling of the bell. Nine strokes would indicate a man had died; six signaled a woman's death; and three strokes indicated a child had perished. At times, short, quick strokes followed the traditional number to broadcast the age of the deceased person. During the funeral, the church bell rang steadily while the people followed the coffin to the cemetery. At nine o'clock each night, the bell announced the day was over. Guests departed homes they were visiting, and persons relaxing in the common bid each other good-night.

The town common, or park, had become the center of a village's life. Cattle once pastured on the green had long before been moved to lands outside the town. Now, village folk lingered to pass the time of day with neighbors or to attend special celebrations, such as watching the militia parade.

The stocks, pillory, and whipping post were also placed in the common. Ridicule was the basis for punishment in the New England colonies. For minor infractions, the culprits were locked into the pillory or stocks with a sign, indicating their crime, hung around their necks. People laughed at a person trapped in the pillory with a sign bearing a capital "D" for drunkard suspended around his neck. A giant "B" signified a blasphemer. The whipping post was reserved for more drastic crimes, and again the town would attend the punishment as further humiliation for the criminal.

Stores and shops sprung up slowly around the common, as well as along the streets throughout the developing town. At first, small villages were generally serviced by wandering peddlers, who made periodic visits to sell their wares. Eventually, the peddler wearied of the transient life and selected a town that had no permanent shop. Thus, the famous New England country store was born.

Like his road-sold products, the former peddler's country store was a hodgepodge of anything and everything. At times this was a necessity, because the country store was the only shop in town. A customer could purchase items ranging from cotton thread to horsewhips, scissors to scythes. The store's aroma was enticing in itself. The smell of spices, candy, and crackers mingled with those of fresh foods and leather, producing an indefinable but distinctive scent. The store was sometimes heated by a wood-burning stove, and the crackling fire added more odors to the small building. Citizens would gather around the stove during the winter to discuss family and village matters, moving outdoors to the store's front porch for their summertime discussions.

Other craftspeople opened shops to provide products for the growing New England towns. Often, if a particular type of craftsman was needed, a town would advertise for the person in larger cities, such as Boston.

An essential service was that of the blacksmith. Every metal object used in the home or on the farm had to be made by hand. The blacksmith's apprentice worked the huge bellows, constructed from several deerskins or even an entire bull's hide, to keep the blacksmith's charcoal fire going. Pounding the red-hot metal with a heavy hammer, the "smithy" forged tools, hinges, and even nails.

The cobbler's shop was another center of activity. People walked almost everywhere in those days, so the demand for new footwear was constant. Often, while the weather was warm and pleasant, people strolled about barefooted, carrying their shoes to put on when visiting a home, shop, or church. In this way, they were able to reduce unnecessary wear and tear on their footgear.

Shoes and boots, too, had to be manufactured by hand. The products were truly custom made. A customer placed his bare foot on a sheet of leather, and the cobbler drew the outline on the sheet. The craftsman then cut out the shoe base and molded other pieces for the top portion. He worked holes into the leather with an awl and sewed the lower and upper portions together. The needle was a hog's bristle, and the thread had been strengthened and waterproofed by working beeswax into the material.

Farmers living outside the town usually provided their own leather. They killed an animal, such as a deer, and then brought the hide to a tannery so that it could be made into leather. Tanneries were generally far from town, because the village residents did not like the unpleasant odors that drifted from the building.

As the towns grew and the people prospered, families discarded their crudely constructed furniture and purchased more fashionable pieces for their homes. Therefore, a visit to the joiner's shop was necessary. A joiner was a person who built objects by "joining" wood together. Generally, these were small, ornamental pieces, such as expertly carved chair legs or decorative paneling around a fireplace. However, as the demand for larger furniture—drop-leaf tables that could be stored in a small area or fancy cabinets—increased, the joiner worked on all types of carpentry. After 1700, he became known as a cabinetmaker.

Surprisingly, the cabinetmaker's tools have not changed drastically since colonial times. He used planes, augers, and spring-pole lathes. All the tools were hand driven. Also, only the actual cutting edges of the tools were constructed from metal. Although the colonial cabinetmaker worked more slowly than modern cabinetmakers, the former could build anything that can be produced today. In fact, even though English cabinetmakers were considered the finest in the world, colonial cabinetmakers were soon turning out products that matched the best from England.

Still more craftsmen arrived in the towns. The potter's shop provided earthenware utensils. Needing only a potter's wheel, powered by a foot pedal, and a supply of clay, he fashioned bean pots, mugs, and dishes. A whitesmith sold tinware, such as dippers and strainers for cooking, as well as candleholders, foot warmers, and tinderboxes. A pewterer produced pewterware for eager customers. Because few colonists had enough money for what they called "plate," silversmiths operated shops only in large cities, such as Boston.

Travel to cities like Boston or from town to town was accomplished by three means of transportation: foot, horseback, and boat.

The early roads were originally paths formed by Native Americans. Movement along these narrow routes could only be done on foot or on horseback. But the early colonists devised an efficient method. Because horses were scarce, two travelers often used only one horse. Obviously, the animal would soon tire, so the "ride-and-tie" plan was formulated. One person would ride the horse a planned distance, while the second individual walked that same route. The rider, upon reaching the destination, tied the horse and walked to the next agreed-upon point. Meanwhile, the walker arrived where the horse was waiting, and then he or she rode the horse, passing the walker and tying the horse at a second place. That person would again continue walking. This procedure allowed each traveler a chance to rest. Even the horse had a breathing spell while awaiting the walker.

The first roads to be planned and built were the "mast roads," so-called because they were constructed to accommodate tall trees that were timbered and used for masts on English ships. The roads were straight and wide enough to allow carts to move along them, but they rarely went where ordinary people wished to travel. Following one might lead an individual to a dead end, deep in a forest. Therefore, township roads, leading to

44

other villages or cities, were built. But these roads went through private land, and each farmer routed them where he wished. The road might curve far to the west to avoid a pasture, then suddenly veer to the east to bypass a cornfield. The owner also placed gates wherever he needed them. Journeying along such roadways was a slow and lengthy process. Not only did the road twist and bend, but a traveler had to continually dismount from his horse, open the gate, lead the horse through, bolt the gate, and—finally—mount the horse once more.

Rivers and the ocean, where accessible, provided faster travel. Fat-bellied shallops were most popular. These resembled round, stubby rowboats and were used by individuals and sometimes employed as ferries. The ferry from Boston to Newtown (called Charlestown today) was a shallop. But the craft was so small that it transported only people. If a person on horseback wanted to travel from Boston to Newtown or the reverse direction, the rider would sit in the boat, but his horse would be tied to the back of the ferry and swim behind.

Other, larger ships were being built, forming the basis for a growing American industry. There seemed to be an endless supply of timber, traveling along the mast roads, so ship construction was cheap. American sailing vessels were soon importing foreign products and exporting the colonists' furs, salt fish, and, of course, lumber. Shipowners in Boston and Salem became wealthy families, with fleets of ships crisscrossing the oceans of the world. Their sons and daughters attended the best private schools and colleges.

However, youngsters from ordinary families often had to make do with whatever education was available. Many farm children learned what they could in the home. A few towns had dame schools, in which the young pupils were taught the catechism, the Lord's Prayer, and the alphabet from the hornbook. This learning tool was not an actual book, but merely a piece of paper with the alphabet printed on one side and the Lord's Prayer on the other. The paper was placed between two pieces of horn, scraped so thin that they were transparent. Other hornbooks had paper attached to a wooden paddle and protected by horn. The very simple schools drew or carved the letters into the wooden paddle, or battledore.

Even though education was skimpy, comparable only to what is learned in the primary grades today, the business of learning these rudiments was a serious one. Discipline was strict. A teacher would not hesitate to use a switch on a misbehaving student. The pupils wrote their lessons on birchbark with a "plummet" of lead. This writing device was real lead, not the graphite mixture found in today's pencils.

Some lettering used by the colonists would confuse a modern student. For example, the ancient Anglo-Saxon letter called "thorn" was printed as a *y* but pronounced as *th*. Therefore, if you saw *ye* on a piece of paper, you would pronounce it as *the*. Also, colonists wrote a long *s* that looked like an *f*. The letter was placed anywhere a small *s* would be found except at the end of a word. Thus, if you encountered the word *treffes* in your reading, you would know it was *tresses*.

In larger communities there were a few more advanced schools, called Latin grammar schools. These were privately financed, and the course of study focused on the reading, writing, and speaking of Latin. Latin was considered the language of learning. In 1636, a minister named John Harvard donated all his books and half his money to start Cambridge College. Others also gave books and money, and the oldest institution of higher learning in the United States—Harvard College—was founded. Here, in a school designed to prepare men for the ministry, the students were expected not only to recite their lessons in Latin but also to hold their conversations in that language, too.

Education, whether it was by firelight in a small cabin or in the halls of Harvard College, was important to the New Englanders. Massachusetts was the first colony to enact a law requiring all villages with fifty householders to employ a teacher of reading and writing, and every town of a hundred families to establish a grammar school. Thus, the public school system as we know it today in the United States was born in 1647.

The heritage passed down to us from the New England colonies is therefore truly important and diverse. From the founding of the first colony, through the hard work and self-sacrifice, to the desire to educate all, the New England colonists provided us with goals and attitudes that are still present in our lives.

3

The Mid-Atlantic Colonies

The Mid-Atlantic Colonies—started by the Dutch and later settled by the British, Scandinavians, and Germans—were the melting pot of nationalities. Each new wave of colonists brought native skills and customs that blended with those already here, creating a different but richer life-style for the colonists.

New Netherland

The Dutch, like the Spanish in the Southern Colonies, arrived with no intention of remaining here permanently. They had been attracted by Henry Hudson's reports of the vast supply of furs in what is now upper New York State. In 1614, Dutch colonists founded an outpost, Fort Orange (where Albany today stands), for the sole purpose of having a trading post to obtain the valuable furs from the Indian tribes of the region. Trinkets were offered in exchange for beaver skins by the colonists, who lived in dugouts or huts. If the Native Americans refused the almost worthless trinkets, the men would barter with brandy and guns. Little thought was given to the consequences of these actions, because the greed for furs was so great.

Meanwhile, other Dutch colonists were squatters on what is now the island of Manhattan. In 1626, the Dutch traded about twenty-four dollars' worth of goods to gain possession of the land they called New Amsterdam. The Dutch colony, New Netherland, now stretched from New Amsterdam in the south, along both sides of the Hudson River Valley, to as far north as Fort Orange. Peter Minuit, who had maneuvered the deal for New Amsterdam, was named the director-general of New Netherland.

Encouraged by his underhanded dealings in the purchase of New Amsterdam, Minuit "bought" both sides of what is now Delaware from the Native Americans on those lands. The price? A few drinks and a handful of cheap jewelry. In 1638, Minuit brought in two shiploads of Swedes and Finns. The Swedes constructed Fort Christina where Wilmington, Delaware, presently stands. Needing immediate shelter, they built the type of home they knew best. Rough logs, still sheathed in bark and with notched ends, were stacked horizontally to form the walls. A side wall log would be set in place, followed by one for the end wall, so that the notches of each timber rested on one another. By doing this, the builder kept the space between the logs in the same wall as small as possible. The thin gaps were then packed, or "chinked," with clay and moss. Thus, the Swedes introduced the prototype of the traditional log cabin, used by colonists and settlers throughout the early years of our nation.

The Dutch West India Company, which controlled New Netherland as the London Company had financed the Virginia colony, wanted to encourage more people to settle on their land. Therefore, huge tracts of land were given to wealthy men known as patroons. The rich patroons acted like miniature West India Companies. They advertised for and financed the voyages of families in Holland that wished to emigrate to New

Netherland. These farmers and tradesmen then had to work to pay back their trip and land expenses. The system was similar to that which existed during the Middle Ages, when a serf was owned by the feudal lord. Perhaps the most famous patroon was Kiliaen Van Rensselaer. Today, the city of Rensselaer, New York, stands on a portion of the large estate the man owned.

If all colonists brought traditions and customs from their home country, the Dutch were even more adamant that their new land would resemble the old. For instance, a small tidal inlet in New Amsterdam was converted into a short canal resembling the canals left behind in Holland. A cobbled lane ran along each side, and bridges spanned the canal. Docking and unloading small boats was easier in the canal, so this became a favorite trading spot for businessmen. Ironically, the site is close to the present Stock Exchange on Wall Street, where today's financiers gather to trade and sell. Later, the canal was filled in with dirt and became Broad Street.

The homes, too, appeared to have been transported across the sea from Holland. Most were brick or frame houses with brick ends. The roofs were thatched. Later, because of numerous fires, the roofs of the high, narrow homes were covered with curved, red tiles. The roofs did not extend to the end walls of the building, but rather the walls were built higher than the roof, with triangular peaks that had a series of indentations, like steps. This was not merely an ornamental addition, but also a means of preventing chimney fires. The chimneys were wide and had steps built inside them. Young boys would scramble along the steps in the peaked walls and then descend into the chimney in order to clean the collected soot and grime.

Decoration was important to the Dutch colonists. The exterior walls of their homes bore testimony to that quality. At times, black bricks were used to create ornamental designs. At other times, initials or dates were constructed right into the walls by using colored bricks, stones, or ironwork.

The features of the homes reflected the fact that the Dutch

colonists were a social people. For example, each house had a Dutch door, with upper and lower halves that opened individually or together. This allowed the Dutch *huys vrouw*, or housewife, to chat with her friends and neighbors through the opened top part; the closed bottom portion kept out the stray dogs and pigs that wandered the streets. The door always had a large brass knocker that was kept polished as if to invite callers to come tapping on the door.

Another aspect of the Dutch colonists' home encouraged the relaxed gathering of people. Directly outside the door, a low, wide platform of brick or wood was built. Two benches, one on each side of the door, faced each other. On warm evenings the men would sit there, smoking their pipes, while the women knitted. Passersby were invited to join the family for a few minutes or several hours. The step on which the benches rested was called a *stoep*. Modern houses often have the same platform—perhaps a bit higher—and have inherited a variation of the Dutch name—stoop.

The condition of the *stoep*, as well as the gleaming door knocker, betrayed another characteristic of the Dutch colonists: cleanliness. Not only was the brass knocker polished daily, but the *stoep* was swept and often scrubbed each day. The interior of the house was equally spotless. The windows sparkled, and fresh linen curtains were hung each week. Floors were scrubbed, then sprinkled with clean sand. Although most of the inside was dazzling white as the result of a fresh application of whitewash, many exposed wooden beams and rafters were also scoured to almost pure white.

The low-raftered rooms were airy and filled with polished tables and large chairs. The ample-sized seating accommodations were needed because the Dutch tended to be heavy people. One of the most important items in the home was a large cupboard, called a *kas*. This was brought to the home by the bride, who had already stocked it with the needed linens. A new visitor to a Dutch home might wonder about the apparent lack of beds. Didn't the family members sleep? Indeed, they slept in beds built into alcoves that were closed off by doors during the day. Often, once the person was nestled into the soft feather bed and covered with a huge quilt, the same doors were locked from the inside. This is comparable to climbing into a cupboard and sleeping with the doors closed and locked.

The fashionable homes of the more prosperous Dutch colonists always had one room, a "best room," which even the family did not use except for a special event like a wedding, christening, or funeral. This concept of a special room, maintained in clean readiness for a family occasion, spread throughout the colonies. Even into the 1950's, some American homes had a parlor reserved for only the most important happening or visitor.

Guests were always surrounded with much food to warm their welcome. One reason the Dutch colonists were such ample people was because they loved to eat. Meals were cooked in large, open fireplaces decorated with blue-and-white tiles depicting biblical scenes. Cookware similar to that used by other colonists hung near the fireplace, but the utensils included one unique item: a large, hinged waffle iron. Unlike the English colonists, who never buttered their bread, the Dutch enjoyed hot waffles smothered with melted butter, as well as cakes and pastries made with generous doses of butter. Their crullers and doughnuts were fried in deep fat—often melted butter—to a golden brown crispness. Guests in a Dutch home were often served *olijkoeck,* a doughnut filled with raisins, apples, and citron. Cake and pastries were so enjoyed by the colonists that bakeries were already operating in New Amsterdam by 1656. One enterprising manufacturer devised a cookie mold in the shape of a hornbook. In school the youngster learned his letters, then ate them.

An important staple of the Dutch diet—as of all the colonists—was corn. Hasty pudding was made by boiling cornmeal in milk. The same cornmeal was also an ingredient in samp porridge. This mixture, made with pork or beef and vegetables, was cooked slowly for three days. The crust became so thick that the porridge was lifted from the pot in a solid piece.

Hornbook.

Other meals featured game birds such as passenger pigeon and wild turkey. Seafood included oysters and lobsters. The Dutch were famous for their cheese, so this food was made and eaten in large quantities. Usually, the colonists grated the cheese, believing that this improved the flavor. And, as was typical for many colonists, extravagant amounts of beer, wine, and brandy were often consumed.

There were numerous occasions to drink. For a people who so enjoyed eating, imbibing, and socializing, a natural outlet would be celebrations and festivities. On December 5, the Eve of Saint Nicholas, the adults presented gifts to the youngsters in honor of the saint who was supposed to reward well-behaved children and punish the bad. Saint Nicholas and gift-giving, blended with the English colonists' version of Father Christmas, producing the now-familiar Santa Claus.

New Year's Day was a most important event for the Dutch. Families would dress in their finest clothes and visit friends and relatives to begin the new year on a cheery, optimistic note. Other holidays included May Day, when maypoles were set up; Shrovetide; and Pinkster Day, which might have been called Prankster Day, for it was a time of tricks and merrymaking.

Even if there was not a special day, the Dutch enjoyed themselves in all types of weather. Ice skating had journeyed with them from Holland, where the frozen canals became winter thoroughfares. Even though Holland was completely flat, the Dutch were the first to introduce the sport of sledding down a hillside.

The children also wanted diversion during their summer days. Toy manufacturing did not begin in the colonies until the mid-eighteenth century, so toys had to be improvised. A boy's favorite possession was his jackknife, with which he made toys, such as a whistle from a willow branch or a top. Top-whipping was a favorite game. Once a top was spinning, the players whipped it with a whiplash to see who could keep it spinning the

longest. The dexterity needed would be equal to that of working a yo-yo.

Youngsters also pitched horseshoes and played marbles. The traditional games of tag and blindman's buff were enjoyed, as was kite flying. Dutch children especially liked knuckle-bones, a game played with sheeps' knuckles. Girls had their dolls, often carved by hand from wood or made from cornhusks or rags. However, the children, like the adults, were adept at making their own fun, so they were able to use these impromptu toys with great enjoyment.

With all the eating, drinking, and fun in Dutch life, a person might form the mistaken impression that New Amsterdam was in a constant party mood. As much as the Dutch enjoyed good times, however, they approached the business portion of their lives with complete seriousness. After all, New Amsterdam was the trade center of the entire New Netherland colony. The rivers teemed with little sloops, or *vlie,* boats that transported the materials needed by the upriver colonists and brought grain and furs downstream from the outposts.

The wheat and corn were shipped to the mills to be ground. The practice of harnessing wind power as an energy source was brought by the Dutch from the old country, so huge windmills dotted the hills of New Amsterdam. Two varieties of mills were used. The "smock" mill is the more familiar one. The building rested firmly on the ground, and the four vanes, or arms, turned slowly in the wind, revolving a wheel inside the mill that crushed the grain kernels. If the wind direction shifted, the cap, or top part, of the mill could be twisted so the sails again caught the breeze. The second kind of windmill was the "post" mill. The body was like a small house set above the ground on a post. Should the wind change course, the entire building was swiveled so that the arms were turned by the wind.

Furs arriving in New Amsterdam were either stored by the merchants to be shipped abroad or purchased by furriers in New Amsterdam. The custom of wearing fur clothing had

A wooden grain shovel.

grown in Europe during the early seventeenth century, and there was a ready market for the colonists' pelts. Numerous "hatters" produced the popular beaver-skin hats either for customers in the colony or for export.

In addition to hatters, bakeries and other small shops operated in the ground-floor levels of the houses. All the Dutch women were not busy scrubbing and polishing their homes, because many of them operated small stores. In fact, those busy housecleaners had created another market demand—brooms. The most efficient were the birch-split brooms, invented by the Native Americans. Because three evenings were needed to make a good birch broom, a rural industry in upper New Netherland and New England developed.

As night fell over New Amsterdam, the men and women returned to their homes for a fine meal and possibly an evening of sitting on the *stoep*. The streets were not totally dark, because every seventh house was required to hang a lantern outside. Homes situated between the lanterns placed candles in protective holders for additional light. The semidark cobblestone streets were patrolled nightly by eight watchmen carrying hefty wooden rattles. The guards periodically announced the time and the weather. If a criminal was spotted, the patrolman whirled the large rattle above his head, hoping the clacking noise would scare the culprit and alert other watchmen and citizens to come to the guard's assistance. The *rattel-wacht,* or "rattle-watch," might well be considered the beginning of the highly trained New York City police force of today. Thus, protected by rattle bearers, the Dutch colonists climbed into their alcoves, locked the cupboard doors, and pulled the quilts about them. As the men, women and children slept, they dreamed happily of a bright new day.

New York

But the new day was a dismal one. On May 11, 1647, Peter Stuyvesant, the new director-general of New Netherland, arrived in New Amsterdam. During the next seventeen years, the peppery old man with a wooden leg brought many positive changes to the colony. Stuyvesant, a pastor, had a small church built for himself, as well as the town's first schoolhouse. He created a fire department, established a hospital, and made an uneasy peace with the Indians, who were justifiably upset over their mistreatment. Seeing that New Sweden and its main city, Fort Christina, were virtually helpless, the fiery Stuyvesant took over the settlement without any resistance and added the land to New Netherland.

Although Stuyvesant tried to reach an agreement with the English colonies surrounding New Netherland, he failed. Bitter feelings between England and Holland gave the English an excuse to attack New Netherland.

On August 23, 1664, four British warships sailed into the harbor of New Amsterdam. Peter Stuyvesant was eager to engage in battle, but the people wisely refused to support his suggestions. Even the average colonists realized their village was outclassed by British war equipment. So, in spite of Stuyvesant's fussing and fuming, the settlement surrendered without the English firing a shot, just as New Sweden had peacefully accepted Stuyvesant's takeover. The Duke of York, brother of the English king Charles II, was made proprietor of the colony, which he renamed New York. The town of New Amsterdam became New York, also.

Although the name had changed and New Amsterdam was now an English possession, the flavor remained solidly Dutch. Despite the efforts of the British, the people continued their Dutch habits and even spoke their native language. In an attempt to change this, the English insisted that Dutch not be spoken in the schools. One schoolmaster found a successful way to enforce this rule. Each day, he gave a metal disk to the first boy who slipped and spoke Dutch. This metal piece was passed to the next student who lapsed into Dutch. The Dutch word for blunder is *bok*. Thus—in all probability—the phrase "passing the buck," meaning to hand some unwanted responsibility to another person of lower rank, came into existence. In this case, the passing of the metal disk ended with the schoolday. Whoever held the piece at that time was thrashed soundly by the schoolmaster.

But whippings by teachers or laws passed by the British had little effect. For nearly the next one hundred years, the English New York might just as well have retained the name of New Amsterdam. The genial, fun-loving, hardworking Dutch colonists, who so enjoyed eating and socializing, possessed still another character trait: stubbornness.

Pennsylvania

While the English proprietors were having difficulties with the willful Dutch, the Church of England was suffering religious rebellion from the Quakers, just as the church had experienced previously with the Separatists and Puritans. The peaceful Quakers were one of the most persecuted religious groups in late-seventeenth-century England. The Quakers believed they must do what their consciences bid them. For example, they were fully convinced that war was wrong, so they refused to fight in the military services. For this action, the dissenters were beaten and thrown in prison.

Their strongest supporter, a Quaker himself, was William Penn, the son of a highly regarded British admiral. Using his father's contacts, Penn met the nobles who were making settlements in America. Undoubtedly, this was when he first formed the idea of a Quaker colony. The spark flared into a burning desire when Penn was imprisoned for speaking out against war. Upon his release, he worked actively toward that goal. A totally new settlement had to be formed for his Quakers, because the group was being mistreated in other New World colonies, such as Massachusetts.

King Charles II owed Penn's father a large sum of money. When his father died, Penn informed the king that he was willing to take a land grant in America as payment for the debt.

The king agreed, pleased not only to have the financial obligation erased but also to be getting rid of the Friends, as the Quakers called themselves. Presenting Penn with the land, located west of the Delaware River and between the present states of New York and Maryland, King Charles II named the region Pennsylvania, or "Penn's Woodlands."

On October 29, 1682, William Penn landed on Pennsylvania soil. The Quakers dug caves into the banks of the Delaware River for temporary shelter and immediately began Penn's planned city, Philadelphia. Penn had created the name himself, for he wanted one that meant "The City of Brotherly Love."

Philadelphia was laid out in neat, rectangular blocks, with streets intersecting at right angles. From the very beginning, sections were set aside for public parks. William Penn's government was founded on the Quaker faith. It granted complete religious freedom and the right to vote for every man. It also reserved capital punishment for only murder and treason.

Philadelphia grew rapidly, without a starvation period such as the other colonies had endured. The Quakers, true to their convictions, soon began speaking out against social injustices. In April 1688, the Germantown Friends Protest against slavery was presented at their monthly meeting. This is the earliest antislavery document in America. Twenty-four years later, the Pennsylvania Assembly passed a law prohibiting the importation of new slaves and urged any Quakers who owned slaves to free them. The Quakers were also among the first colonists to provide education for both black and Native American children.

The new homes were simple and functional, as dictated by the Quakers' tastes. Inside the brick house, each of the four ground-floor rooms had a fireplace angled into a corner. All fireplaces led into the same, wide chimney. A narrow stairway, set between the front and the back rooms, climbed to the attic. The windows were constructed so they would slide up and down, unlike most windows in other colonists' homes, which were either stationary or opened out like a door.

During the winter months, Quakers placed hot coals in the brass containers of their bed warmers.

New arrivals continued to pour into Philadelphia. By 1690, the population had grown to 4,000, topped only by Boston's 7,000 residents. However, Philadelphia was destined to become the largest city of the English colonies by the mid-1700's.

Along with the people came prosperity. Because Philadelphia had direct access to the Atlantic Ocean, shipping and trade were the mainstays of the business world. Ships could be built in the colonies for about one-third the cost of constructing a vessel in Europe, so many customers at the Philadelphia shipyards were from foreign countries.

The hulls of the oceangoing ships followed the British design, no matter how many or what sails the craft bore. The shape was rather like a tub, with a balky stern. A "head," or hornlike structure, jutted from the bow. However, for their own use, the shipbuilders experimented with sail and hull patterns to see if they could develop sailing ships with more speed and the same cargo capacities. Fewer square sails were hung horizontally to the ship's body, and more fore- and aftsails were strung parallel to the hull. Gradually, the ships became narrower and sharper in order to slice the waves cleanly.

The ships docking in Philadelphia brought a new wave of colonists. Although Germans had arrived the year after the Pennsylvania colony had been founded, they now emigrated in ever-increasing numbers. The conditions under which they crossed the Atlantic and waited permission to disembark are reminiscent of the deprivation suffered by black slaves during their voyages from Africa. Some Germans, who had little or no money, literally sold themselves and their sons into labor for the passage money. Because many people were crowded into cramped, dirty areas aboard ship, disease often spread throughout the passengers. Hundreds died at sea, and the survivors often had to wait weeks in quarantine once they reached American shores. And, if the new colonists were forced to set at anchor, neither the shipowners nor shore authorities would provide food. The already weakened immigrants had to survive on what they could buy with their meager funds or on any provisions that charitable Philadelphians might donate to them.

Although a number of Germans remained in Philadelphia, the majority moved directly into the back country of Pennsylvania to settle on farms. These people were called the Pennsylvania *Deutsch,* or Germans. Over the years, however, mispronunciation caused them to be known as the Pennsylvania Dutch. Industrious and thrifty, the Germans became the best farmers in all the colonies. Their barns were larger and more intricately constructed than their homes. The immense structures had stone ends and were built into south-facing banks. The planning was excellent. First, nestling a barn into a hillside meant protection from the winds and greater warmth in the floors. For further insulation from the harsh Pennsylvania winters, the Germans stacked cornstalks against the exposed portions of the foundation. Being built into the bank gave still another advantage to the barn's function. Hay wagons could drive along the ridge of the bank and directly onto the upstairs floor to unload their cargoes.

Not only did the German farmers need wagons to carry their hay, but they also required transportation for their products to the coastal markets. The Pennsylvania *Deutsch* in the Conestoga Valley devised a vehicle that became known as the Conestoga wagon. The same thorough precautions that had gone into their barn design were executed in the wagon. Heavy loads would have to be carried, and most roads twisted and climbed steep inclines. If a load shifted, the wagon would tip over. Therefore, the twenty-four-foot body was boat-shaped. It sloped upward at the front and rear, and the sides curved outward. This arrangement caused the cargo to settle toward the bottom and the middle of the wagon body, providing better equilibrium. A framework of arches extended along the body length, and homespun cloth was draped over the supports to cover the valuable produce.

Not only were the wagons functional, they were also aesthetically pleasing. The sides were painted a brilliant blue; their

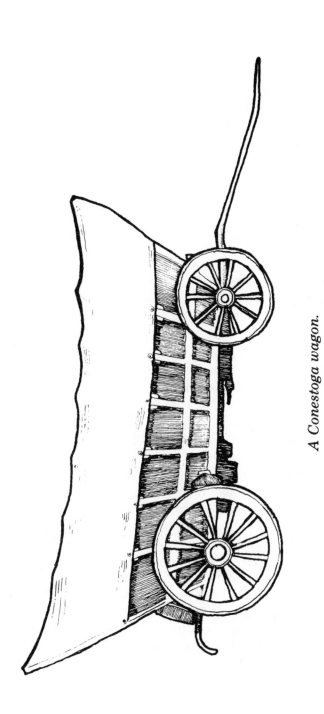

A Conestoga wagon.

trim was bright red. The colorful wagon body contrasted sharply with the white canvas topping. Drawn by six or eight horses, wagon-and-team stretched for about sixty feet. In long convoys of fifty or one hundred wagons, the German farmers jingled and clinked their way along the rutted roads and into history. This Conestoga wagon was the model for the covered wagons that the pioneers would later use in their westward trek.

Almost as an afterthought, the German farmers gave attention to their homes. At first, they adapted the Swedish log cabin built at Fort Christina, because construction was fast and the needed materials were at hand. In fact, the trees needed to be cut anyway to clear the fields. The Germans made improvements in the basic model. First, they leveled the tops and bottoms of the logs so they would fit together more snugly. Also, the log ends were cut off to give the house a neater appearance.

By the mid-1700's, the Germans were building houses with thick stone walls. Again, their home construction was aiding their farming. Using the stones from the fields now served double-duty on the farm, because the fields had to be cleared of the many rocks and boulders. Having learned the value of building their barns into banks, the Germans constructed their homes into the hillsides. The ingenious colonists then devised still another way to make their houses into farm helpers. The homes were built over springs so that the cellars were cooling rooms for milk, vegetables, and meat.

Although the outside appearance was trim and neat, there was little decoration on a German house. Many homeowners placed an iron silhouette of a Native American on the roof to advertise the fact that they had purchased their land from the original owners. The families seemed to be saving their ornamentation for inside the home. The kitchen was considered the main room, because everyone always gathered there. Decorative wooden paneling covered the walls, and the stairway leading into the kitchen had an elaborately carved banister. Color

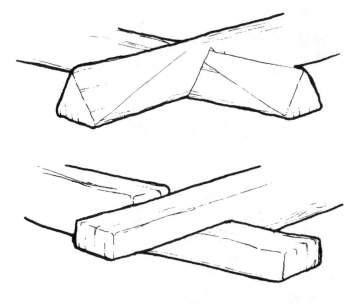

Log ends used in cabin construction.

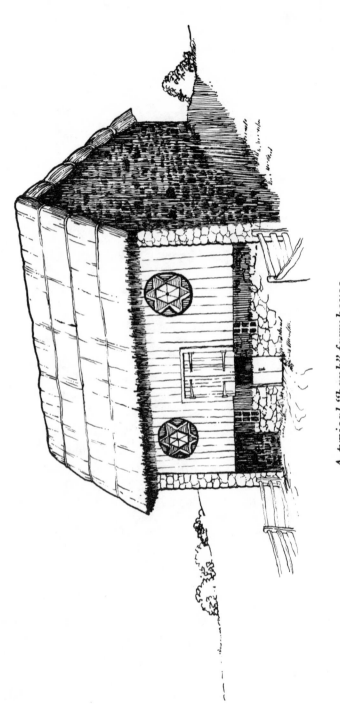

A typical "bank" farmhouse.

was added by painting the furniture with bright, cheerful designs of birds and flowers, particularly tulips.

Many Germans who settled the hills of Pennsylvania belonged to strict religious sects such as the Mennonites, who founded Germantown. Even today, pockets of these groups exist throughout Pennsylvania, maintaining many beliefs and customs of the first colonists.

While the Germans who had moved into rural Pennsylvania were making their contributions to the colonial way of life, those who had settled in Philadelphia were also giving of their talents. Glassmaking in the colonies had been a complete failure. The Dutch manufactured some glass in New Amsterdam during the 1650's, and Massachusetts had imported a few German glassmakers, but neither venture had proven successful.

Not until 1739, when a German colonist, Caspar Wistar of Philadelphia, and his son, Richard, operated their factory, was glass manufacturing profitable. Along with regular window glass and goblets, the Wistars produced a specialized side product of window glass and bottles with brass buttons embedded in them. In 1765, another Pennsylvania *Deutsch,* Heinrich Wilhelm Stiegel, who preferred to be called "Baron" Stiegel, became the greatest American glassmaker. Through his improved methods, he perfected a clear flint glass, molding the material into bottles and goblets of rose, amethyst, blue, and green hues.

Glassmaking required great skill and strong lungs. The basic mixture of lime (from oyster shells), sand, and soda or potash was melted down in an arched furnace of brick. A craftsman, using a long metal blowpipe, scooped a blob, or "gather," of molten glass onto its tip. As he puffed through the blowpipe, the bubble grew in size. Then, by swinging and maneuvering the mass, he achieved a general shape. At times, the glass cooled and had to be reheated, so that the glassmaker could continue to mold the bottle.

Due to a problem in the glass-blowing process, free-blown bottles bore an indelible identification mark. As the glass cooled, it became firmly attached to the end of the blowpipe. It could only be detached by snapping the bottle off at the lip, leaving a jagged edge around the top. To finish his work, the bottlemaker used an iron punty, or pontil rod, which was dabbed into melted glass and attached to the outside bottom of the bottle. The pontil rod served as a handle by which the glassblower could hold the bottle in the furnace, or "glory hole." The reheated top again became pliable and could be smoothed. The long iron punty was broken from the base, leaving a "pontil scar," or glass bump. Many years later, this bump would enable bottle collectors to estimate more exactly the container's age.

Window glass, also, had a telltale mark. The process of making window glass began in the same way. The glassblower transferred the mixture to the rod and, by spinning the rod between his hands, flattened the molten glass into a wide disk. When the disk was thin enough, the man broke off the rod, leaving the bump of glass in the middle. This scar became known as the "bull's eye" and was considered a flaw. Today, people who own old homes with windowpanes that have a bull's eye highly value the antique glass.

Still growing, the colony of Pennsylvania moved into the eighteenth century. The Scotch-Irish colonists, far different in temperament from the peaceful Quakers, settled the Cumberland and Juniata valleys. For some reason, these people hated the Native Americans and viewed them only as savages. As would be expected, the Indians retaliated with frequent attacks. The Scotch-Irish decided that the log cabins the Swedish colonists and, later, the Germans had used were ideal for their mode of living. They continued to build them long after others had discarded the idea.

Due to the constant danger of attack, the Scotch-Irish grouped their log cabins around a water supply and built a wall surrounding the small settlement. The wall for the fort was made with sharpened logs and had one or several blockhouses for additional protection. The blockhouses were two-story log structures in which the second level overhung the lower one.

Care was taken to smooth the exterior as much as possible, so that attackers would not have a foothold to climb the building. The upper level had loopholes through which rifles could be fired. If the structure had a door, there was only one, and that was heavy and thick. Frequently, the entrance to the blockhouse was on the upper story. Entry was gained by climbing a ladder which could then be hauled into the blockhouse.

A misconception exists about this frontier colonist's clothing. Pictures always show them wearing fringed leather shirts. In reality, the Scotch-Irish colonist wore a rough linen shirt in warm weather and a linen-wool shirt during the winter. Leather was much too uncomfortable when the material became wet, and the colonists were outside in all kinds of weather. The long shirt was fringed and hung to the waist. Open in front, the garment was secured by a belt. Other images of the colonists' appearance are correct, however. They wore long leggings and high moccasins, the tops of which were tied around the leg just below the knee. During the winter, dry leaves or deer hair was placed into the moccasins to keep the feet warm. Strapped to the belt on the right was a tomahawk; a sheathed knife was inserted on the left side.

The Scotch-Irish as a group were outspokenly independent and often hostile to outsiders. Years might pass before they were fully accepted by the colony's population. Their major contribution—whiskey—was accepted more readily.

In the early part of the eighteenth century, Philadelphia lost its great leader when William Penn died. Five years later, in 1723, a Bostonian left his native city and moved to Philadelphia. Benjamin Franklin adopted the city and showered its people with affection. By 1729, he was the editor and publisher of the *Pennsylvania Gazette,* and he used the paper as a means to enlighten the residents about the needs of their city.

Newspapers were slow in coming to the colonies. The "Father of American Newspapers," Benjamin Harris, published the first newspaper to appear in the colonies. On September 25, 1690, *Publick Occurrances* sprang forth from a Boston coffee house. The paper had little time to build circulation, however, because the governor of Massachusetts suppressed the publication after only one issue. On April 24, 1704, John Campbell, a New England postmaster, issued *The Boston News-Letter* from the back room of his home. For fifteen years, this was the only newspaper in Boston, achieving a circulation of three hundred copies.

One reason for the lack of newspapers was the scarcity of paper. In 1690, William Rittenhouse, a Dutch papermaker in Germantown, Pennsylvania, organized the first paper mill. Paper was made from linen rags boiled in lye. They were then placed in flat molds and pressed into sheets. But a shortage of linen always existed in the colonies. Some newspapers even urged their readers to save old linen rags for the paper mills. Another reason for the scarcity of newspapers was that until 1750, all printing presses, type, and ink had to be imported from England. Therefore, setting up a print shop was an expensive matter.

The early newspapers were single sheets of paper, folded in half and about the size of a contemporary magazine. The content dealt mainly with what was happening in England. Some papers reprinted the latest letter the editor had received from England, but this letter was weeks, sometimes months, old. Yet, people were eager for any word about what was happening in the old country. Just as in today's newspapers, advertisements were important. Advertisements were placed by stores announcing the latest imports they had received. Other notices told of farms, horses, and even slaves for sale. Almost every newspaper carried ads about horses that had strayed or had been lost or stolen. Other than that, the only news related to the colonies was announcements about the arrivals and departures of ships, as well as their respective cargoes.

Benjamin Franklin was not the first editor to realize a newspaper's potential impact upon its readers, but he did use his paper and other publications to motivate people to eliminate civic problems. Under Franklin's leadership, Philadelphia led the colonies in social reform. A hospital for both the medically and psychologically ill was set into operation, along with a prison that was more humane than any in the world. Franklin helped organize a fire department and urged that the streets of Philadelphia be paved. He also devised a plan by which the poor would receive medical treatment, and established a circulating library.

Eventually, Franklin became the spokesperson for all the colonies. In 1765, the English Parliament passed the Stamp Act, which required tax stamps for newspapers, legal documents, and other printed material. No action by the mother country had so enraged the colonists. A Stamp Act Congress met later that year, and the delegates formulated their protests against the tax. Representatives were sent to England. In February 1766, Benjamin Franklin stepped before the House of Commons and eloquently presented the colonists' objections. The Stamp Act was repealed one month later, and the prospect of rebellion was diminished. As the years passed, however, more injustices were enacted against the colonies, and the cry for independence rose again.

By June 1776, as the Second Continental Congress convened in "The City of Brotherly Love," Philadelphia had changed drastically from the days when the community was a haven for the Quakers and other persecuted religious sects. No one can be certain how William Penn would have felt when his city became the birthplace of the Declaration of Independence—a document that set into motion the War for Independence. Fiercely against war, Penn might have been dismayed. On the other hand, the Revolutionary War was fought for freedom, and Penn was equally strong in his belief that people should be free. And for a nation, self-rule is the ultimate freedom. So, perhaps the fact that colonial times ended on July 4, 1776, in a city founded to allow freedom is a most fitting tribute to William Penn.

The End of the Colonies

The official date for the end of the colonial period was the signing of the Declaration of Independence. But, in actuality, colonial times had ended long before, when the people in all the colonies realized they must stop focusing merely on the problems of Massachusetts or thinking only about what was happening in Virginia. The difficulties belonged to them all, and everyone had to unite to find the solutions.

Perhaps this is the greatest message we can get from reading about how the colonists lived. To know our history and take pride in it is important, as is the understanding of how much of our contemporary lives have been affected by the original colonies. However, the spirit of cooperation and the drive toward a successful conclusion that was exhibited by the colonists is necessary in the nation today, as we struggle against different but equally serious problems that threaten the United States.

Index

DATE DUE			